VICTORIOUS

EMOTIONS

Journal

*A 30-DAY JOURNEY TO REWIRE
YOUR BRAIN*

Wendy Backlund

Victorious Emotions Journal
© copyright 2017 Wendy Backlund, Igniting Hope
Ministries www.ignitinghope.com

Cover Design and Interior Formatting by Reddovedesign.com
Editors: Melissa Amato and Darlene Edskerud

ISBN 978-0-9863094-8-9

Please note that the author's publishing style capitalizes certain
pronouns in Scripture that refer to Father, Son, and Holy Spirit
and may differ from other publishers' styles.

Disclaimer

This journal and its brain exercises for living with victorious emotions is not written for the clinically depressed or emotionally tormented, although this may help. I have created this journal and my book *Victorious Emotions* for those who cannot break the cycle of the draining, negative emotional interference that restricts us not only from rising to our full potential, but from living a joy-filled, abundant life. This journal is designed to equip people with practical, life-transforming steps to break habits of bad beliefs and draining emotions and to live a victorious and empowered life.

I am not a doctor or therapist, and I do not advise quitting any medications prescribed by your doctor or therapist without their consent.

Note: This journal is intended to be used with my book Victorious Emotions.

Table of Contents

Note From The Author

This journal is a valuable resource designed to help you apply the truths presented in my book *Victorious Emotions*, but it's not essential for reaping the benefits of the book. The journal is designed for convenience so that every day you'll have the five brain exercises and room for journaling right in front of you. This is your chance to take what you've learned and apply it to your life. This journal was created to help prompt you into a new life.

Many psychiatrists or counselors can help you deal with the past events that have started negative emotional issues in your life, but that is not what the book *Victorious Emotions* or this journal is about. This journal is a tool to activate the five brain exercises that will offensively create new, happier, healthier emotional responses. The goal is not stopping negative emotions, but creating new pathways in the brain that create an

"

AS A SINGLE FOOTSTEP
WILL NOT MAKE A PATH
ON THE EARTH, SO A
SINGLE THOUGHT WILL
NOT MAKE A PATHWAY
IN THE MIND. TO MAKE
A DEEP PHYSICAL PATH,
WE WALK AGAIN AND
AGAIN. TO MAKE A
DEEP MENTAL PATH,
WE MUST THINK OVER
AND OVER THE KIND OF
THOUGHTS WE WISH TO
DOMINATE OUR LIVES

-

HENRY DAVID
THOREAU

"

involuntary release of healthy emotions. Think about it – we do not usually consciously choose our emotions. No one decides to be overwhelmed on purpose or tries to work up that emotion. It is a reflexive, involuntary response based on subconscious belief systems that have created deep pathways in our brains. So this journal is an opportunity to offensively and intentionally create massively deep pathways of faith, hope, and joy. It is an emotional muscle-building system to strengthen your healthy responses to everyday life.

Unfortunately, many people only focus on removing negative emotions from their lives. They think the goal is to stop feeling whatever negative emotion happens to be driving them at the moment. I have noticed that the fight against negative, draining emotions tends to be reactive. For example, a negative circumstance may occur which triggers a negative emotional response like fear, hopelessness, shame, depression, anger, or self-pity. As maturing Christians, we try to fight off those emotions, knowing they are not helpful or Christlike. Unfortunately, trying to defend ourselves from the overwhelming chemical release that is already rushing through our system can be a losing battle. The religious premise is that it is sinful to have these bad emotions, and when they crop up, we must squash them, hide them, or pretend they do not exist. The premise for this journal is not about fighting negative emotions, but taking time to create new victorious emotions that can begin to take over our lives.

You may be in a season of depression or fear while starting this journal. Give yourself grace to have those emotions – don't fight them; instead commit to taking time every day to do the five brain exercises to begin to rewire your brain to have a positive default response to life. As Henry David Thoreau once said, "As a single footstep will not make a path on the earth, so a single thought will not make a pathway in the mind. To make a deep physical path, we walk again and again. To make a deep mental path, we must think over and over the kind of thoughts we wish to dominate our lives."

I pray that each one of you who begins this journey will experience the empowering love and grace of God each time you pick up this journal. May you be strengthened by God to experience the fullness of joy and peace that is our rightful inheritance in Christ.

Blessings on your journey,

Wendy

How To Use This Journal

Practical Steps

As you begin this journey of rewiring your brain for victorious emotions, it is important to do each exercise for the full thirty days. The thirty days create a habit in the brain. If you do not have the capacity to do all five exercises at the same time for thirty days, choose one or two exercises to implement for the full thirty days. Then go back and complete the other exercises. As you start these exercises, keep in mind that the first week may take longer as you learn how to do the different exercises. If you are doing all five exercises, set aside 45 to 60 minutes per day for the first week. As the weeks go on, it will become faster for you to do the exercises. Give yourself grace, and know this will get easier and easier as you practice. It is important that you do not just accomplish the exercises, but that you actually have an emotional reaction to each exercise.

Each brain exercise has space for you to journal your emotions and thoughts. In my own exercises, I often do the imagining by writing out a positive scenario and then picturing it over and over in my imagination. Then I journal what I see each time God adds to the picture. Writing down how the exercise affects your emotions is a good tool for articulating and verbalizing what God is doing in you. Please do not get discouraged if it is hard to imagine or feel an emotion at first. Remember, you are building a new muscle both with the imagination and also in your emotional responses.

Variations On Using This Journal

Although I recommend doing the exercises every day, do not allow yourself to quit just because you miss a day or two. If all five exercises are too overwhelming and time consuming, spend a month on just one or two exercises and then do two more the next month. You may not be able to do the exercises in 30 consecutive days, but as long as you spend thirty days on each exercise, it will help you build new pathways in the brain. However, the closer together the thirty days are, the more impactful the results will be. Just like working out physical muscles at the gym needs a measure of consistency, so does building pathways in the brain.

Doing four squats is better than nothing, but if you want to see real results, you need to continue to do squats. If you can only devote three or four days a week on one exercise, it is still better than doing nothing at all. Decide what will be the most successful plan for you personally, and then do it! You can always go back and spend another month on the other exercises.

Checking Your Progress

I have included a checklist to help you keep track of how many days you have spent on each exercise. Remember, it is more effective to work on one exercise at a time rather than doing a different one each day. Focusing on the same exercise/exercises consistently over 30 days is more beneficial than spreading all the exercises out. The goal is to complete one exercise fully rather than doing a different exercise every day.

Making It Work For You

Begin this journey to rewiring your brain in faith, believing Holy Spirit will guide you and let Him adapt this journal so it fits your personality and learning style. Do not get legalistic about the exercises. You do not work for them – they should work for you according to your personality. Celebrate your progress, and never stop starting. The goal is to actually make these exercises a life habit. We can never have too much hope and joy! These five brain exercises and prompts are just a way for you to start. We encourage you to continue to explore with Holy Spirit and go deeper and deeper with your encounters.

Personally, I like to keep things simple and will focus on the same imagined goal over and over until I feel like I own it. I know it is working for me when it becomes an automatic response in real life.

Victorious Emotions Self-Assessment

Take a moment before you begin your 30-day journey to assess your default emotions by rating yourself on the following page and recording the date under the Pre-Exercises Self-Assessment. After completing the exercises in this journal for at least 30 days, re-assess yourself and record your results under the Post-Exercises Self-Assessment.

Pre-Exercises Self-Assessment

Date: _____

Results: _____

Rate each question from 1 to 5 using the scale below:
1 - Never, 2 - Seldom, 3 - Sometimes, 4 - Often, 5 - Always

1. People tell me I am joyful. _____

2. I have hope in the face of unfortunate events._____

3. Joy is my default emotion. _____

4. My thoughts are positive when I'm falling asleep. _____

5. I affect other people's emotions more than they affect mine. _____

6. I look for opportunities to celebrate my progress. _____

7. I intentionally cultivate thankfulness and gratitude. _____

8. I wake up and joyfully expect a good day. _____

9. I dream and imagine my life with Jesus intervening in my (seemingly) hopeless situations. _____

10. My moods aren't affected by external events or people. _____

11. I don't feel responsible for the happiness and success of other people. _____

12. I don't believe every thought I have. _____

13. I don't get stuck inside my head. _____

14. I don't suffer from low-grade depression. _____

15. I don't experience stress or anxiety. _____

Post-Exercises Self-Assessment

Date: _____

Results: _____

Rate each question from 1 to 5 using the scale below:

1 - Never, 2 - Seldom, 3 - Sometimes, 4 - Often, 5 - Always

1. People tell me I am joyful. _____
2. I have hope in the face of unfortunate events. _____
3. Joy is my default emotion. _____
4. My thoughts are positive when I'm falling asleep. _____
5. I affect other people's emotions more than they affect mine. _____
6. I look for opportunities to celebrate my progress. _____
7. I intentionally cultivate thankfulness and gratitude. _____
8. I wake up and joyfully expect a good day. _____
9. I dream and imagine my life with Jesus intervening in my (seemingly) hopeless situations. _____
10. My moods aren't affected by external events or people. _____

11. I don't feel responsible for the happiness and success of other people. _____

12. I don't believe every thought I have. _____

13. I don't get stuck inside my head. _____

14. I don't suffer from low-grade depression. _____

15. I don't experience stress or anxiety. _____

FIVE BRAIN EXERCISES

———

To Rewire Your Brain for a Happier You

Brain
Exercise
ONE

Rehearse

and

Reimagine

OVERVIEW

When the will and imagination are in opposition, the imagination always wins. The human brain has more faith in what it can see than in what it wants to do. So if you want to be a happier person but cannot imagine yourself as happy, then no matter what you do, it will not bring any long-term emotional change. People usually only rehearse the past, but it is time to live out of your future. Instead of rehearsing past negative events or reactions, rehearse God encounters or personal testimonies of what you want God to do again. Be selective. Choose what you want to see more of in the future.

A God encounter could be a time when you felt emotionally connected to God, had a life-changing revelation, or experienced a worship or prayer time when you were very aware you were connected to God, spirit to Spirit. You need to start emotionally rehearsing your God encounters, testimonies, successes, and happy moments of your day in your mind until you have an emotional response. It is the repeated release of happy emotions with intentional thoughts that begins to build a new stronghold. This exercise will help you train your brain to look for happy moments you have experienced.

CHECKLIST

EXERCISE ONE

Day 1	Day 11	Day 21
Day 2	Day 12	Day 22
Day 3	Day 13	Day 23
Day 4	Day 14	Day 24
Day 5	Day 15	Day 25
Day 6	Day 16	Day 26
Day 7	Day 17	Day 27
Day 8	Day 18	Day 28
Day 9	Day 19	Day 29
Day 10	Day 20	Day 30

"

IT IS THE REPEATED
RELEASE OF HAPPY
EMOTIONS WITH
INTENTIONAL
THOUGHTS THAT
BEGINS TO BUILD A
NEW STRONGHOLD

"

JOURNAL
EXERCISE ONE

G o back and remember your God encounters and replay them in your brain. Choose a favorite God encounter, testimony, happy moment, or success and spend ten minutes imagining it happening again. It may help to write it down as you remember it happening. Try to picture details and re-experience the emotions you had during that experience. I highly recommend reimagining the same event for at least ten days in a row in order to convince your brain of the reality of that event. The goal is to train your brain to believe that these kinds of experiences are now normal. If you are rehearsing a God encounter, be open to God adding new details and enlarging on it.

Victorious Emotions Journal

Victorious Emotions Journal

Victorious Emotions Journal

Victorious Emotions Journal

Brain Exercise TWO

Celebrating

the

Positive

OVERVIEW

To create victorious emotions like joy, peace, and hope, we must realize they are not a personality trait that some people have and others do not. Some people seem to be blessed with a more natural talent for positive emotions, but we all have the ability to build strongholds for victorious emotions. We are not victims to how our brains are functioning. We can decide to think new thoughts that create strongholds of joy. Victorious emotions should be a byproduct of being born again. The only reason they do not manifest in all Christians is that many have not renewed their minds enough yet to produce victorious emotions. Because Christians fear becoming prideful, we often try to be neutral about our talents and successes. This is a mistake. We need to give ourselves permission to celebrate who God has made us. We need to allow God to celebrate our baby steps and to receive encouragement from Him. Healthy and happy people tend to attribute good events to who they are and believe that good is more permanent than adversity or evil. However they tend to attribute negative events as transient and not their fault.

Each day, intentionally look for and write down positive events in your life. As you do this, you will train your brain to look for something different than what it currently believes and create new strongholds. This may seem difficult at first. Ask God for grace to help you see what you previously could not see. Don't be afraid to write down things that seem insignificant. Remind yourself that you are building a new muscle, so do not judge the things that come to mind. For example, you might write: "I said no to cake." We often condemn ourselves for eating a cookie, instead of focusing on the positive and celebrating that we said no to cake. If you failed at something, find something in the failure to celebrate and focus on that.

CHECKLIST
EXERCISE TWO

Day 1	Day 11	Day 21
Day 2	Day 12	Day 22
Day 3	Day 13	Day 23
Day 4	Day 14	Day 24
Day 5	Day 15	Day 25
Day 6	Day 16	Day 26
Day 7	Day 17	Day 27
Day 8	Day 18	Day 28
Day 9	Day 19	Day 29
Day 10	Day 20	Day 30

"

YOU HAVE BEEN
RELEASED FROM
PERFECTION AND
GIVEN PERMISSION
TO BE IN PROCESS

"

JOURNAL

EXERCISE TWO

Write down four victories or positive things you did today or yesterday. (If you do this in the morning, you will use yesterday's events; if you do this in the evening, use the events of the current day.)

In your imagination, replay one of these events and celebrate it over and over again. Picture yourself and God dancing, laughing, and celebrating. Take time to hear God congratulate you and encourage you.

Brain
Exercise
THREE

Cultivating Hope

and

Thankfulness

OVERVIEW

EXERCISE THREE

Many of us don't experience thankfulness because we are thinking about what has not happened yet or what happened in the past. We are anchored either in the future or the past, rather than the present. We are unconsciously preparing and worrying about the future. Or we are rehearsing our past so often that it feels like the present. Searching for things to be thankful for causes us to realign ourselves with the present moment and enjoy the good that we are currently experiencing. It is scientifically proven that when we reflect on what we are thankful for, it boosts the serotonin (the chemicals that make our brains happier) in our brains. Furthermore, simply looking for things to be grateful for increases the production of serotonin in the brain. Being thankful releases stress and renews our soul.

Being thankful helps us lose our fear for the future because it reminds us of God's faithfulness. This is especially relevant if we tend to prepare for bad to happen and are fear based. If we have faith for bad things to happen, we will want to control everything and everyone. We will spend emotional energy trying to prepare for a future that has not happened. When you begin to feel emotional energy loss, ask yourself: "Is this worth expending my energy? Can I afford to spend my energy resource on this?" Ask Holy Spirit: "What belief is draining my energy? What do I need to believe to re-empower myself and restore my peace?"

We must believe that hope can be cultivated and taught. Rehearsing testimonies of God's faithfulness and goodness will begin to build a stronghold of hope in your brain. Create an emotional attachment to these two truths: 1) God always has a solution, and 2) He always makes a way for me to regain what has been stolen or lost.

Our brains will give weight and value to what we focus on and to what has the most emotional response. While reading the Bible, every time you see God deliver or bless someone, create an emotional response by declaring, "This is my Father! And He also delivers and blesses me!" It is important to rehearse and celebrate every time we encounter His goodness. This will build a muscle of hope. Picture Him doing it for you, or through you, until it becomes real to you. It is important to stop reading the Bible for information only. It needs to become revelation. It is not revelation until it changes how you view and emotionally respond to life and circumstances.

CHECKLIST

EXERCISE THREE

Day 1		Day 11		Day 21	
Day 2		Day 12		Day 22	
Day 3		Day 13		Day 23	
Day 4		Day 14		Day 24	
Day 5		Day 15		Day 25	
Day 6		Day 16		Day 26	
Day 7		Day 17		Day 27	
Day 8		Day 18		Day 28	
Day 9		Day 19		Day 29	
Day 10		Day 20		Day 30	

"

BASKING IN AND SUSTAINING THE EMOTION OF GRATEFULNESS QUICKENS THE PROCESS OF BUILDING A HAPPY BRAIN

"

JOURNAL

EXERCISE THREE

Write down five things you are thankful for. Spend at least one minute reimagining one thing on the list, and bask in the emotion of gratefulness.

Now imagine an area of hopelessness being invaded with God's goodness and supernatural power. (Hint: Think of how you used to worry, but do it in a positive way. Imagine a future filled with God's goodness and the supernatural happening.)

_____

_____

_____

_____

_____

_____

_____

_____

Brain Exercise Three // Cultivating Hope and Thankfulness

Brain Exercise Three // Cultivating Hope
and Thankfulness

Victorious Emotions Journal

Brain Exercise Three // Cultivating Hope and Thankfulness

Brain Exercise Three // Cultivating Hope and Thankfulness

Brain
Exercise
FOUR

Release
Responsibilities

OVERVIEW

Release yourself from false responsibility. You are not responsible for other people's emotions, reactions, decisions, or successes. You are responsible to be on the journey of living from your resurrected spirit and bringing the revelation and presence of God. You are responsible for changing the way you think and for renewing your mind, which in turn will benefit all who come in contact with you. We all may be a part of the answer for someone's freedom, but no one is the complete answer. We each reveal a facet of Christ or carry a breakthrough anointing that will help others on their journey to wholeness and freedom. But as soon as we feel responsible for someone's whole life, then we set ourselves up for failure. If you feel inadequate when trying to help someone or if it is draining to help them, you either need new beliefs about yourself or you are trying to do something you were not called to do. Usually it is a measure of both. Having healthy boundaries means you know how to protect yourself without rejecting people. Boundaries should never be erected out of fear – anything built around fear will carry a wrong spirit. Boundaries should be built out of a confident self-esteem that recognizes our value to be taken care of. It is being okay with taking time to have fun and to restore our own soul. But if we think we are someone's savior, then we will take on false responsibilities for them. This will cause us to sacrifice our own future for theirs.

Realize that not every emotion is yours. I have always been empathetic with sensing how others feel. I've felt other people's emotions so deeply it made me want to avoid them because I felt responsible to make them feel better. I lived under an unconscious coping mechanism where I would avoid certain places or hurry out of them without thinking about why. For example, I used to feel uncomfortable and anxious when I went in certain stores. I was picking up on the atmosphere and the emotions of the people inside the store. Likewise, airports or anywhere else that engendered high levels of stress for people were uncomfortable for me because I was taking on the emotions of the people there as my own. If you are a feeler, it is tempting to take them on as your own or feel responsible for helping make people feel better. But feelers are supposed to be supernatural releasers of new and healthier atmospheres. They are created to bring joy and hope and to release the negative emotions to God. When you feel something different as you walk into a new setting or location, verbalize what the feelings are and release them to God.

CHECKLIST
EXERCISE FOUR

Day 1		Day 11		Day 21	
Day 2		Day 12		Day 22	
Day 3		Day 13		Day 23	
Day 4		Day 14		Day 24	
Day 5		Day 15		Day 25	
Day 6		Day 16		Day 26	
Day 7		Day 17		Day 27	
Day 8		Day 18		Day 28	
Day 9		Day 19		Day 29	
Day 10		Day 20		Day 30	

"

YOU ARE NOT ANYONE'S SAVIOR OR EVEN YOUR OWN

"

JOURNAL
EXERCISE FOUR

Look back on your day and write down any times when you started feeling other people's emotions and made them your own. Picture how you could have released a new atmosphere or emotion instead of being the one influenced.

For example, is there an adult whose success you feel responsible for? Are you working harder at it then they are? If yes, picture yourself handing the responsibility back into their hands. Now picture yourself handing that person and your emotions (like fear, worry, or frustration) into God's hands.

Victorious Emotions Journal

Brain Exercise FIVE

Dream and Build a

Framework for the

Supernatural

OVERVIEW

God released a strategy to me to begin creating a mindset for empowering strongholds. I fix my eyes on the unseen substance of God's Kingdom. You can build empowering strongholds by spending time dreaming with Holy Spirit and picturing the substance of the spirit realm and Kingdom of light. For instance, what would happen to darkness if you were literally light? Imagine the power of words bringing life to dead things. See angels working on your behalf.

Connect with your spirit. It has total peace and a sense of dominion. It is in perfect accord with God. It is the real you. Imagine it getting larger and more confident. It hears God perfectly because it knows it has perfect relationship with Him. It has senses, feelings, and wisdom apart from the natural mind or natural soul. It feels hopeful, at peace, full of passion, love, and grace. It emanates from within you, touching your body, soul, and mind. It emanates a sense of fulfillment, safety, and security. It is not influenced by natural circumstances because it is only moved by the unseen realm of God's love and goodness. Focus on what your spirit is feeling, sensing, and seeing. Allow your spirit to expand and emanate its perfectness. Allow yourself to experience your spirit's sense of wholeness and security. Allow your spirit to influence your natural mind and natural emotions. Allow the joy of the spirit to overflow with abandonment, expecting only good to come to you.

As you declare these statements out loud, picture what they would look like in your life:

» I am aware of the unseen realm and bring supernatural wisdom and authority to things and circumstances.

» My spirit is one with God and therefore feels no shame, fear, or hopelessness.

» Self, you are more spirit than flesh. Your identity rests in who you are in Christ, not who you are emotionally, physically, or experientially. You have all things in Christ.

» Because I am light, I can overcome darkness, sickness, and depression. People are sent into realms of the spirit as they get near me. They have God encounters and are instantly healed!

» My supernatural life comes so easily, and it feels almost like I am floating in a whole new dimension. There is such joy and laughter all around me! I awaken feeling refreshed and aware of the unseen realm.

» My body is full of energy and is perfectly healthy.

» I feel loved and empowered and trusted by God. I radiate His Presence as I meet with people. I bring violent love encounters to people that instantly free them from the consequences of their pasts.

For more information on why we make declarations, see the book Declarations by my husband, Steve Backlund.

CHECKLIST

EXERCISE FIVE

Day 1		Day 11		Day 21	
Day 2		Day 12		Day 22	
Day 3		Day 13		Day 23	
Day 4		Day 14		Day 24	
Day 5		Day 15		Day 25	
Day 6		Day 16		Day 26	
Day 7		Day 17		Day 27	
Day 8		Day 18		Day 28	
Day 9		Day 19		Day 29	
Day 10		Day 20		Day 30	

"

WHILE YOU DREAM,
ALLOW YOUR
SPIRIT'S JOY TO
OVERFLOW WITH
ABANDONMENT,
EXPECTING ONLY
GOOD TO COME TO
YOU

"

JOURNAL
EXERCISE FIVE

Spend ten minutes dreaming with God. Find a comfortable, distraction-free place and close your eyes. To start, pick a scenario to dream about and stick to it for a full thirty days. Try to see and feel as many details as possible. Use the same dream over and over until it is easy and feels possible. In order for this dream to rewire your brain, I recommend choosing one scenario and re-imaging it for the full 30 days. Make up your own dream or choose one of the following scenarios:

Scenario One

Invite Holy Spirit to give you healthy pictures of how life should be lived. Close your eyes and imagine yourself walking in peace and confidence during circumstances that usually bring stress or fear. Picture God blessing your life in finances, emotions, anointing, favor, and talent. Picture doing what you love to do and people supporting and valuing you while you do it. See yourself receiving different blessings during your day.

Scenario 2

Ask Jesus to let you see yourself as you really are – as confident, powerful, and always making wise decisions. Imagine waking up in the morning full of energy and expecting great things to happen in you and through you. Picture yourself having perfect peace while doing everyday things. Picture yourself shifting atmospheres everywhere you go. See yourself healing the sick and witnessing for Christ.

Scenario 3

Spend time allowing Holy Spirit to reveal the substance of the spirit realm and Kingdom of God. For instance:

» Imagine what would happen to darkness if you were literally light.

» Explore the possibilities of being seated in heavenly places.

» Imagine the power of words bringing life to dead things.

_____

_____

_____

_____

_____

_____

_____

_____

_____

_____

_____

_____

_____

_____

_____

_____

_____

_____

_____

_____

Victorious Emotions Journal

Brain Exercise Five // Dream and Build a
Framework for the Supernatural

_____

_____

_____

_____

_____

_____

_____

_____

_____

_____

_____

_____

_____

_____

_____

_____

_____

_____

ABOUT THE COVER

The cover of this book holds much significance to me. I chose the image of the moon because God began to speak to me that our emotions are similar to the tides of the ocean. There are high or low tides according to the position of the moon. The ocean does not work to have a low tide or high tide; it is determined by the gravitational pull of the sun and moon. Likewise, our emotions are released in full force or downgraded by the gravitational pull of our subconscious beliefs. He began to show me that our unhealthy emotions cannot be changed by trying to make ourselves feel something else. Rather, we build a new "solar system" of beliefs based on the Spirit and the Word of God.

Negative emotions overtake our lives when we have not built a strong enough inner ("solar"/emotional) system. Healthy belief systems based on the Word of God restore the victorious emotional ecosystem intended by God. The goal of this book is not to focus on negative emotions but to build a default system that will always return us to joy.

In the same way that the phases of a new moon are gradual, the process of changing our beliefs will take time. We must relax as the "old moon" of our beliefs begins to grow smaller, and then watch the miracle of the "new moon" begin to enlarge.

ADDITIONAL
RESOURCES
From Wendy & Steve

VICTORIOUS EMOTIONS

This book gives powerful, practical strategies to live out Romans 12:2, which says to be transformed by the renewing of the mind. The word "renewing" in the Greek means renovation. This book is about renovating and reconstructing the pathways and strongholds of our thinking. It explores how our brains create certain belief systems and how to intentionally create new ones. The goal of this book is not to focus on eliminating negative emotions, but to build a tidal wave of victorious emotions that are pulled into our lives as easily and surely as the ocean tides will appear every day. It is time to be overtaken by emotions that lead us into victory!

LIVING FROM THE UNSEEN

This book will help you identify beliefs that block the reception of God's blessings and hinder our ability to live out our destiny. This book reveals that 1) Believing differently, not trying harder, is the key to change; 2) You cannot do what you don't believe you are; 3) You can only receive what you think you are worth; 4) Rather than learning how to die, it is time to learn how to live.

ENCOUNTER: AN ACTIVATION OF YOUR SPIRIT

Wendy Backlund directs listeners through this 38-minute, focused, meditative invitation into the Presence of God using relaxation tools that build a constant awareness of their spirit and God. Like the healing river flowing from the temple door in Ezekiel 47, Wendy welcomes us to step into the deeper waters of God and pursue His face as we encounter Him spirit to Spirit. Lie down, relax, close your eyes, and engage as Wendy equips you to have your own life-transforming experiences and encounters with God. This is not merely a listening CD, but rather an experiential one, designed to lead us into face-to-face, transformational encounters with God.

VICTORIOUS MINDSETS

What we believe is ultimately more important than what we do. The course of our lives is set by our deepest core beliefs. Our mindsets are either a stronghold for God's purposes or a playhouse for the enemy. In this book, fifty biblical attitudes are revealed that are foundational for those who desire to walk in freedom and power.

POSSESSING JOY

In His presence is fullness of joy (Psalm 16:11). Joy is to increase as we go deeper in our relationship with God. Religious tradition has devalued the role that gladness and laughter have for personal victory and kingdom advancement. His presence may not always produce joy; but if we never or rarely have fullness of joy, we must reevaluate our concept of God. This book takes one on a journey toward the headwaters of the full joy that Jesus often spoke of. Get ready for joy to increase and strength and longevity to ignite.

YOU'RE CRAZY IF YOU DON'T TALK TO YOURSELF

Jesus did not just think His way out of the wilderness and neither can we. He spoke truth to invisible beings and mindsets that sought to restrict and defeat Him. This book reveals that life and death are truly in the power of the tongue, and emphasize the necessity of speaking truth to our souls. Our words really do set the course of our lives and the lives of others (Proverbs 18:21, James 3:2-5).

LET'S JUST LAUGH AT THAT

Our hope level is an indicator of whether we are believing truth or lies. Truth creates hope and freedom, but believing lies brings hopelessness and restriction. We can have great theology but still be powerless because of deception about the key issues of life. Many of these self-defeating mindsets exist in our subconscious and have never been identified. This book exposes numerous falsehoods and reveals truth that makes us free. Get ready for a joy-infused adventure into hope-filled living.

DIVINE STRATEGIES FOR INCREASE

The laws of the spirit are more real than the natural laws. God's laws are primarily principles to release blessing, not rules to be obeyed to gain right standing with God. The Psalmist talks of one whose greatest delight is in the law of the Lord. This delight allows one to discover new aspects of the nature of God (hidden in each law) to behold and worship. The end result of this delighting is a transformed life that prospers in every endeavor. His experience can be our experience, and this book unlocks the blessings hidden in the spiritual realm.

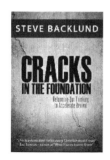

CRACKS IN THE FOUNDATION

Going to a higher level in establishing key beliefs will affect one's intimacy with God and fruitfulness for the days ahead. This book challenges many basic assumptions of familiar Bible verses and common Christian phrases that block numerous benefits of our salvation. The truths shared in this book will help fill and repair "cracks" in our thinking which rob us of our God-given potential.

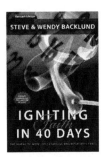

IGNITING FAITH IN 40 DAYS

There must be special seasons in our lives when we break out of routine and do something that will ignite our faith about God and our identity in Christ. This book will lead you through the life-changing experience of a 40 day negativity fast. This fast teaches the power of declaring truth and other transforming daily customs that will strengthen your foundation of faith and radically increase your personal hope.

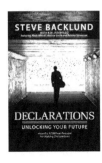

DECLARATIONS

"Nothing happens in the kingdom unless a declaration is made." Believers everywhere are realizing the power of declarations to empower their lives. You may be wondering, "What are declarations and why are people making them?" or maybe, "Aren't declarations simply a repackaged 'name it and claim it' heresy?" *Declarations* answers these questions by sharing 30 biblical reasons for declaring truth over every area of life. Steve Backlund and his team also answer common objections and concerns to the teaching about declarations. The revelation this book carries will help you to set the direction your life will go. Get ready for 30 days of powerful devotions and declarations that will convince you that life is truly in the power of the tongue.

CRUCIAL MOMENTS

This book helps us upgrade how we think, act, and most importantly, believe in those crucial moments when: You feel nervous about speaking in public, Your house is a mess when people come over, A politician whose beliefs oppose yours is elected, You gain more weight than you thought, You don't feel like worshiping and 47 other opportunities for breakthrough.

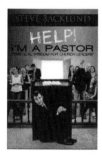

HELP! I'M A PASTOR

This book is practical, revelatory, and humorous, with 50 common scenarios that could cause a pastor to say, "They didn't prepare me for this in Bible school!" *HELP! I'm A Pastor* replaces exasperation with expectation using 80 life and leadership core values to tackle situations including: My People Are Always Late For Meetings, I Am Tempted To Have An Affair, How Transparent Is Too Transparent?, and Pastor, She Is A Jezebel.

LET'S JUST LAUGH AT THAT FOR KIDS!

We all want the best for the young people in our lives. *Let's Just Laugh at That for Kids!* will help you set children up for success by teaching them to replace lies with truth and to take a combative stance against beliefs that try to hold them back. This book invites you into an interactive journey in taking every thought captive with the kids you love. Through these fun, laughter filled pages, we expose twenty common lies kids often believe, and this book helps train them to use "laughter weapons" to disarm the lies. We then use Scripture, declarations, and practical wisdom to reinforce the truth.

THE CULTURE OF EMPOWERMENT

Have you ever been championed by someone? You have likely had times when people believed in you more than you believed in yourself. Their belief in you became a rock to stand on against the waves of insecurity, doubt, and fear in your mind. They were willing to allow you to try something challenging and new under their mentorship, and it caused you to find out there was more in you than you thought. This book by Steve Backlund reveals a solid biblical foundation for living a lifestyle of empowerment. Through empowering people, Jesus set an example for us and revealed the Father's heart in doing so. *The Culture of Empowerment* gives insight and practical tools for championing people as well as developing empowering beliefs about yourself and others.

ABOUNDING HOPE AND JOY CURRICULUM DVD/CD

In this powerful teaching series, Steve and Wendy Backlund impart divine strategies for success that will equip every believer to live with abounding hope and joy. This teaching will break off limits from individuals and position them to be continually transformed by the renewing of their minds. Through laughter, declarations, biblical truth, and revelatory teaching, Steve and Wendy move people into higher perspectives and victorious mindsets.

Audio message series are available through the Igniting Hope store at: IgnitingHope.com All books available on Kindle at Amazon.com

Printed in Great Britain
by Amazon